YOU WILL BE A GREAT FOOTBALLER

You Will Be a Great Footballer

Read Daily for Affirmation Book Series

Walter the Educator

Silent King Books

SILENT KING BOOKS

SKB

Copyright © 2024 by Walter the Educator

All rights reserved. No part of this book may be reproduced in any manner whatsoever without written permission except in the case of brief quotations embodied in critical articles and reviews.

First Printing, 2024

Disclaimer
This book is a literary work; poems are not about specific persons, locations, situations, and/or circumstances unless mentioned in a historical context. This book is for entertainment and informational purposes only. The author and publisher offer this information without warranties expressed or implied. No matter the grounds, neither the author nor the publisher will be accountable for any losses, injuries, or other damages caused by the reader's use of this book. The use of this book acknowledges an understanding and acceptance of this disclaimer.

I pray that you be a great footballer.

For where two or three are gathered together in my name, there am I in the midst of them - Matthew 18:20

YOU WILL BE A GREAT FOOTBALLER

In the dawn's embrace, I rise, with dreams unfurled,

You Will Be A GREAT FOOTBALLER

A vision burning bright, my destiny's twirled.

You Will Be A
GREAT
FOOTBALLER

I lace my boots with purpose, each knot a vow,

You Will Be A
GREAT
FOOTBALLER

To tread the sacred turf, the here and now.

You Will Be A
GREAT
FOOTBALLER

"I will be a great footballer," my mantra bold,

You Will Be A GREAT FOOTBALLER

A promise to myself, a story to be told.

You Will Be A
GREAT
FOOTBALLER

With every sinew, every stride, I'll chase the light,

You Will Be A
GREAT
FOOTBALLER

Through shadows of doubt, I'll emerge in flight.

You Will Be A
GREAT
FOOTBALLER

The pitch, my canvas, where passion will paint,

You Will Be A
GREAT
FOOTBALLER

Brushstrokes of sweat, of courage, no complaint.

You Will Be A
GREAT
FOOTBALLER

With every pass, every dribble, each goal,

You Will Be A
GREAT
FOOTBALLER

I'll carve out my legacy, etch my soul.

You Will Be A
GREAT
FOOTBALLER

On fields of green, where dreams collide,

You Will Be A
GREAT
FOOTBALLER

I'll dance with destiny, side by side.

You Will Be A GREAT FOOTBALLER

From the roar of the crowd, to the silent night,

You Will Be A
GREAT
FOOTBALLER

I'll nurture this fire, burning bright.

You Will Be A
GREAT
FOOTBALLER

I see the game with eyes that gleam,

You Will Be A
GREAT
FOOTBALLER

Each moment a stitch in a glorious seam.

You Will Be A
GREAT
FOOTBALLER

A tapestry of effort, of lessons learned,

You Will Be A
GREAT
FOOTBALLER

For every missed chance, a triumph earned.

You Will Be A
GREAT
FOOTBALLER

In the weight of the ball, the rush of the wind,

You Will Be A
GREAT
FOOTBALLER

I find my rhythm, where the world's rescind.

You Will Be A
GREAT
FOOTBALLER

The echo of footsteps, a heartbeat's call,

You Will Be A
GREAT
FOOTBALLER

In every corner, every play, I stand tall.

You Will Be A
GREAT
FOOTBALLER

Challenges will rise, like waves on the shore,

You Will Be A
GREAT
FOOTBALLER

But I'll meet them head-on, ask for no more.

You Will Be A
GREAT
FOOTBALLER

In the face of defeat, I'll hold my ground,

You Will Be A GREAT FOOTBALLER

With resilience and heart, I'll rebound.

You Will Be A
GREAT
FOOTBALLER

Every practice, a step toward the sun,

You Will Be A
GREAT
FOOTBALLER

Each training, a chapter in battles won.

You Will Be A
GREAT
FOOTBALLER

With teammates beside me, we'll craft our fate,

You Will Be A
GREAT
FOOTBALLER

Through unity and grit, our skills innate.

You Will Be A
GREAT
FOOTBALLER

"I will be a great footballer," a whisper first,

You Will Be A GREAT FOOTBALLER

A growing anthem, quenching thirst.

You Will Be A
GREAT
FOOTBALLER

For glory isn't just the score or fame,

You Will Be A
GREAT
FOOTBALLER

It's the honor, the spirit, the love of the game.

You Will Be A
GREAT
FOOTBALLER

I'll run with the wind, kick with the tide,

You Will Be A
GREAT
FOOTBALLER

With discipline and zeal, I'll stride.

You Will Be A
GREAT
FOOTBALLER

Each whistle's call, each referee's shout,

You Will Be A
GREAT
FOOTBALLER

Will guide me forward, through the bout.

You Will Be A
GREAT
FOOTBALLER

And in moments of quiet, when shadows loom,

You Will Be A
GREAT
FOOTBALLER

I'll find solace in the pitch's bloom.

You Will Be A GREAT FOOTBALLER

For within these lines, my heart finds rest,

You Will Be A
GREAT
FOOTBALLER

In the beautiful game, I'm at my best.

You Will Be A
GREAT
FOOTBALLER

ABOUT THE CREATOR

Walter the Educator is one of the pseudonyms for Walter Anderson. Formally educated in Chemistry, Business, and Education, he is an educator, an author, a diverse entrepreneur, and he is the son of a disabled war veteran. "Walter the Educator" shares his time between educating and creating. He holds interests and owns several creative projects that entertain, enlighten, enhance, and educate, hoping to inspire and motivate you.

> Follow, find new works, and stay up to date
> with Walter the Educator™
> at WaltertheEducator.com

www.ingramcontent.com/pod-product-compliance
Lightning Source LLC
LaVergne TN
LVHW012049070526
838201LV00082B/3872